Printed and Published in Great Britain by D.C. THOMSON & CO., LTD.,185 Fleet Street,
London EC4A 2HS.© D.C. THOMSON & CO., LTD., 2005. ISBN 1 84535 0456

SMELLY

£6.99

HOW DID KNIGHTS OF OLD KEEP IN TOUCH?

CHAIN MAIL LETTERS.

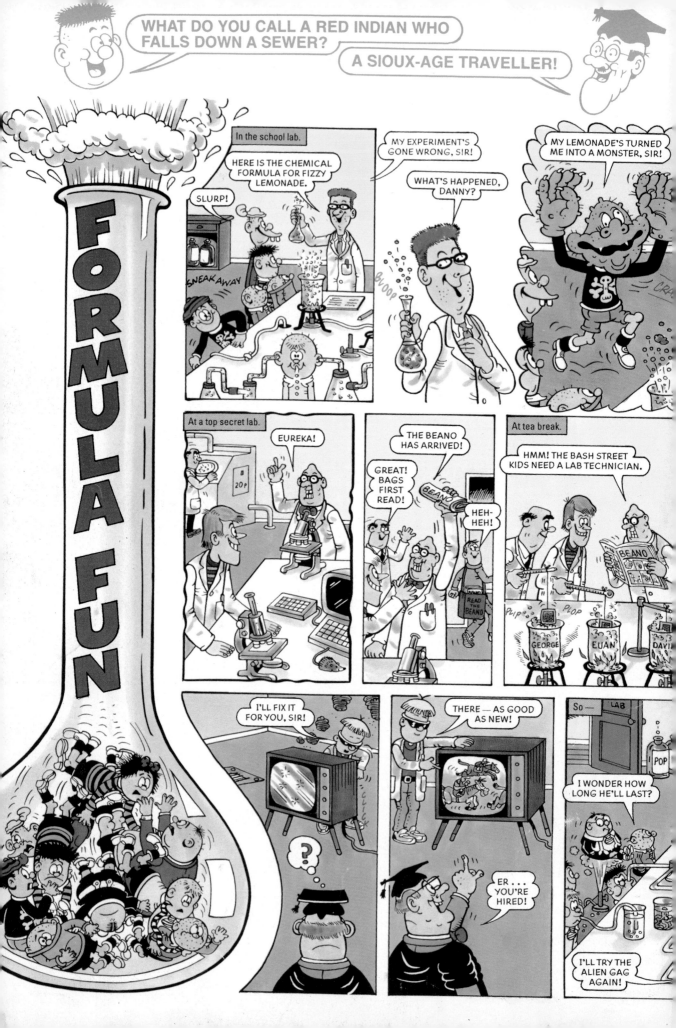

WHAT DO YOU CALL SOMEONE WHO USED TO LIKE FARM VEHICLES?

AN EX-TRACTOR FAN.

AARGH!

SCHOOL

WAVE

FOR YOU!

EH?

I RESIGN!

THUD

LAB TECHNICIAN WANTED — MUST BE CRAZY

THIS SPACE FOR RENT

Later —

SIGH! NOT ONE SINGLE APPLICANT.

LAB TECHNICIAN WANTED — MUST BE CRAZY

THAT'S THE LEGS WORKING OKAY.

PRESS

CLICK WHIRR

HEAD OKAY.

WAVE

Later —

THIS IS A MODEL LABORATORY KNOWLEDGE DISPENSING COMPUTERISED TECHNICIAN — TECHNO FOR SHORT!

GREAT!

TUG

SWOOSH

In Head's study.

OH, BOO! AND I DID WANT TO WATCH OPEN UNIVERSITY!

PUSH OPEN

BOO!

WAIT!

I AM TECHNO!

POP

PING

BOO!

LEAP

PUZZLING! IF YOU ARE ATTEMPTING TO LOOK LIKE AN INHABITANT OF RIGEL III, THEY DON'T LOOK LIKE THAT . . .

. . . THEY LOOK LIKE THIS!

FLASH

AAARGH!

WE'RE GONNA LIKE HIM!

AND I THINK I SHALL LEARN MUCH FROM THEM TOO! SEE YOU IN SEVEN DARKNESSES!

WHAT DO YOU GET IF YOU CROSS A PIG WITH A TREE?

A PORKY-PINE!

EXPERI-MENTAL!

YAHOO! TIME FOR OUR SCIENCE LESSON!

SCIENCE LAB

ZOOM

ZOOM

WAH!

WHEEE

STICKY BUN

TRIP

AHA! A GOOD EXAMPLE OF THIS LAW IS ABOUT TO HAPPEN!

AW, NO!

SPLAT

YOU SEE! THE STICKY SNACK FELL TO THE EARTH'S SURFACE — BUT WHY?

HA-HA! HE'S CLUMSY!

NOT THE LOGICAL ANSWER I WANT!

HUMPH!

HAIRY STICKY BUN

EH?

WHAT?

THESE ARE SIMPLE 'ANTI-GRAVITY' BOOTS! I CONSTRUCTED THEM ONE LUNCH-TIME!

WOW!

PRESS!

PRESS!

RISE

COOL!

DO YOU SEE? I AM NOW FREE OF GRAVITY! THE LAW OF THE EARTH'S PULL!

GASP! DID YOU MAKE ANY MORE PAIRS OF BOOTS, TECHNO?

FLOAT

MOST CERTAINLY! SCAN THE STORAGE SPACE!

HE MEANS THE CUPBOARD!

ER ... STORAGE ... UM ... SPACE?

Soon —

CAN WE TEST THEM, TECHNO?

WHAT DO YOU GET IF YOU CROSS A MICROPHONE WITH A WHEATFIELD?

A CROP IDOL!

OUR SCIENCE LESSON IS MORE INTERESTING BECAUSE OUR LAB TECHNICIAN IS A ROBOT! HE'S CALLED, 'TECHNO'!

TECHNO BEING ASSEMBLED

PLEASE INSTALL YOURSELVES IN YOUR ALLOTED SPACES! THE SCIENCE LESSON IS ABOUT TO BE UP AND RUNNING!

PLESE TELL ME WHICH 'LAW' THIS REPRESENTS, EARTH BEINGS!

EH?

... ERM!

LAW?

SCRATCH!

CHEW!

TUG!

ER ... HO ... HUM!

YOU DO NOT UNDERSTAND THIS BASIC LAW? GASP! MY DATABASE IS AT A LOSS FOR TERMS TO EXPLAIN MY DISBELIEF!

LOOK! SIMPLE! THIS EXPLAINS THE 'LAW OF GRAVITY'!

I SHALL DEMONSTRATE FURTHER!

CUP-BOARD

CHOMP! CHEW!

HMM! NOT HERE ... HERE ... HMM!

WOW!

TOSS

TOSS

Soon —

OBSERVE MY ACTIONS!

AFFIRMATIVE! GO ON!

COME AND JOIN IN, TECHNO!

AHEM! NOT QUITE A SCIENTIFIC EXPERIMENT BUT ... PERHAPS SOMETHING WHICH SHALL PROVIDE MUCH ENTERTAINMENT! HA-HA! OKAY!

THROW

PLOP

CRASH

GRAB

OOPS!

WAHEY! GOOD SHOT!

BOOM!

CLANK

SPLAT

COMB!

MIRROR

WHY DID THE SOLDIER HAVE A FOREIGN STAMP ON HIS FOREHEAD?

HE WAS POSTED ABROAD!

MIND YOUR MANNERS, KIDS

...BAD WEATHER?

In the Dining Hall.

NO — LUNCH TIME WITH THE KIDS!

OOOH! TOO SORE, SIR!

EH?

WHEN ONE IS SITTING NEXT TO 'ERBERT! OW!

BLIND AS A BAT

AHEM!

HEH-HEH!

AND WHEN A LADY AND GENTLEMAN APPROACH A CLOSED DOOR . . . WHAT HAPPENS NEXT?

I TRIP UP SMIFFY . . .

RAISE ONE'S CAP, SIR!

GOOD BOY!

RAZZ!

EEEK!

SCREAM!

I DO LIKE A BICCY! CHOMP!

LIFT OFF

THROW

SPLASH

HOW MUCH IS THAT DOGGY IN THE WINDOW?

YOU'LL GET NO CHANGE OUT OF A DOG POUND.

IT'S ABOUT TIME YOU TAUGHT THIS LOT SOME BASIC MANNERS! DO IT THIS AFTERNOON!

YES, YOUR HEADSHIP!

After lunch.

AHEM! THIS AFTERNOON'S LESSON WILL BE ON MANNERS!

HA-HA!

ONE MUST HOLD ONE'S PINKIE ALOFT WHILST ONE IS DRINKING ONE'S TEA!

. . . AND HE OPENS THE DOOR FOR ME! HAR-HAR!

CRASH!

AAA!

OH, NO!

HAR-HAR!

HEH HEH! THAT TICKLED!

TEA UP, TEACHER!

AHA! DANNY! WHAT MUST ONE DO WHEN GREETING A LADY?

HOW'S THE MANNERS CLASS GOING?

CLASS IIB

OOOOH!

Then —

DRING! TRINNG!

YAHOO!

THE END OF THE SCHOOL DAY!

HOME TIME!

NNNGH! LET ME OUT! LADIES FIRST!

CHORTLE!

HA-HA!

GET OFF!

I WANT AWAY!

TISK! TISK! WHAT AN EXAMPLE OF BAD MANNERS!

WHAT GETS RID OF HORRIBLE, NASTY SUMS?

WEAPONS OF MATHS DESTRUCTION.

SILENCE IS GHOUL-DEN

IT'S TIME FOR CLASS!

NOT YET, TEACHER, THE BELL IN THE SCHOOL CLOCK TOWER HASN'T STRUCK NINE O'CLOCK!

BONG! BONG! BONG!

ONE . . .

TWO . . .

THREE . . .

WOW! THIS'LL WAKE THE TOWER GHOST!

AW! RUBBISH!

YA-BOO!

GHOST?

MOAN.... GROAN.... OOOOO!

EEK! WHAT WAS THAT?

THE GROANS CAME FROM IN HERE!

OOOOH!

MOAN! GROAN!

ZZZZZZ

FATTY!

EH? OH . . . WHAT?

CHORTLE! SO THIS IS WHERE HE COMES FOR A QUIET SNACK BEFORE CLASS!

THERE'S WHY THE BELL DIDN'T STRIKE NINE!

YEAH! I STUCK A PORK PIE ON THE CLAPPER! IT WAS TOO NOISY!

HUH! I KNEW IT COULDN'T HAVE BEEN A GHOST ALL ALONG!

SILENCE

EH? ONLY STRUCK THREE!

HA-HA! SIX SHORT!

OOH! THIS IS A BAD . . . VERY BAD SIGN!

SCHOOL

EH?

In the school library.

COUGH! COUGH!

PUFF

COUGH!

IT SAYS IN THIS ANCIENT BOOK ABOUT OUR SCHOOL — 'ALL WILL BE FINE, TILL THE CLOCK FAILS TO STRIKE NINE'!

WHAT CAN HAPPEN?

the school kitchen.

HA-HA! NOT GHOSTS — THE MICE HAVE BEEN PINCHING OLIVE'S COOKING!

CHORTLE!

GROAN!

MOAN!

OOO!

CHUCKLE! NO SUCH THING AS GHOSTS!

SO YOU'LL GO UP TO THE TOWER AND SEE WHAT'S WRONG WITH THE BELLS, SIR!

ER . . . WELL!

OKAY! I'LL BE BRAVE AND RISK IT! THIS GARLIC WILL KEEP OFF EVIL SPIRITS!

TO THE TOWER

GARLIC SMELL

ZZZZZZZ

EH? I THOUGHT THE BELL STOPPING SHORT OF NINE CHIMES WAS MEANT TO WAKE THE GHOST!

IT SOUNDS AS IF THE GHOST IS ASLEEP!

I'M GLAD I SAVED THIS PIE TILL NOW! CHOMP!

THROW

OOOH! TEACHER!

YIKES!

A SPOOK!

EEK!

THE TOWER GHOST!

WAA!

ALL TRUE!

A STRANGE LOT! I ONLY WANTED TO TELL TEACHER ABOUT THE LUNCHTIME STAFF MEETING! I'VE JUST CLEANED THE CHALK OFF MY BOARD IN MY STUDY FOR THE MEETING!

WIPE

WHEN WERE VEGETABLES FIRST DISCOVERED?

DURING THE CABB AGE!

MEASURING JAPE

In class.

CAN ANYONE TELL ME WHAT THE HEIGHT OF STUPIDITY IS?

ABOUT 1.6 METRES! HAW-HAW-HAW!

NOT FUNNY!

PING

PING

A NICE SOFT LANDING!

OOOH!

TUG!

DID YOU KNOW CUTHBERT'S CONK COULD STRETCH TO 15 CMS!

AND TEACHER'S NECK MEASUREMENT IS JUST 5 CMS!

GLURK!

TUG

MY HEAD'S ONLY 12 CMS!

AND MINE'S 7 CMS STRAIGHT THROUGH!

PULL

AND A MIGHTY 'PLUG TYPE' SNEEZE!

EH?

SPLUDGE

BLAST

AACHOOO!

AND YOU GET!

OO . . . ER! I'M COVERED IN THIS MIXTURE!

HARDEN

OH, NO! THIS STUFF'S GONE HARD! I CAN'T MOVE!

CHORTLE! YOU GET — THE AFTERNOON OFF!

WHAT DO YOU GET IF YOU CROSS A DONKEY WITH AN INSECT?

A BRAYING MANTIS!

TEE-HEE! TODAY WE'RE GOING TO TALK ABOUT MEASUREMENTS!

COO! GREAT!

SNATCH

IT'S GOOD TO SEE YOU'RE SO KEEN ON YOUR WORK!

DON'T BE DAFT . . .

THROW

. . . I'M NOT KEEN ON WORK . . .

ZZZZT

LIFT

. . . I'M KEEN TO GET MY MODEL MOON ROCKET BACK!

GRRR!

GRAB

MEASURING IS VERY IMPORTANT IN COOKING!

TAKE ONE MOUTHFUL OF PEAS!

BLAST

ADD A SOCKFUL OF CHEESE!

SHAKE

THEN A PAIL FULL OF GREASE!

POUR

CLASS II B

But —

EEK!

TRIP
TRIP
WHEE
SOAK SPLAT

LUCKILY TEACHER TOOK 'MEASURES' TO FOIL THE LITTLE DEVILS!

LOOSEN UP!

WHIRR

MELT

WE DON'T MIND A THUNDERSTORM!

GREAT FUN, IN FACT! HA-HA!

HISSS

HISSSS

INSIDE AT ONCE! IT'S SILLY STAYING OUT IN THIS WEATHER!

SCHOOL

Suddenly.

CRACK!

EEK!

WOW!

WAA!

I KNOW . . .

JOTTER

SWOOSH!!

HO-HO! HE'S STILL FULL OF ELECTRICITY!

HE CERTAINLY LEFT A 'MARK' ON OUR JOTTERS!

WHAT'S GOING ON?

TEACHER'S BEEN STRUCK BY LIGHTNING, SIR!

IIB

TAKE HIM TO MY STUDY — AT ONCE!

BZZ

BZZ

WHAT DO YOU CALL A TREE CROSSED WITH WALTER THE SOFTY?

A BIG SAP!

Suddenly.

CRACK!

CRACK!

FZZZZ

WOW! LOOK AT THAT!

WOW! GREAT TRICK, SIR!

A WALKING X-RAY!

HOW'D HE DO THAT?

... PUT THESE RUBBER GLOVES ON TO PROTECT US!

DOH!

WAH!

GRAB

GRAB

LET'S GET TEACHER INSIDE!

In class.

I MUST MARK THESE!

FZZZZ

BZZT!

FZZZ

THIS WAY, SIR!

BZZT!

BLOOP!

JOTTERS

ater.

HMM! HEAD'S TAKING HIS TIME PHONING FOR AN AMBULANCE!

LET'S SEE WHAT'S GOING ON?

NO — I HAVEN'T PHONED THE HOSPITAL YET!

HEAD'S STUDY

I HAD A LOT OF WORK TO CATCH UP ON — AND MY LAMP'S BROKEN!

HA-HA!

OUT OF ORDER

BZZT!

FZZT!

BZZT!

KNEEL HERE

CHORTLE! ONE OF THE HEAD'S BRIGHTS IDEAS!

The Bash Street Kids Fat Club

I SHOULD'VE DONE THIS LONG AGO!

SCHOOL TUCK SHOP

THUD! THUD!

BUT WHY, SIR?

WE USE THE TUCK SHOP ALL THE TIME!

EXACTLY! THAT'S WHAT'S TURNED YOU INTO A CLASS OF FAT PORKERS.

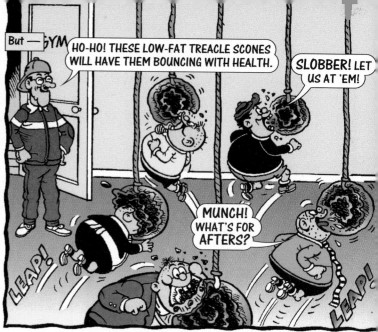

WHAT INSTRUMENT DO DOGS PLAY?

LEAD GUITAR!

KIDS BEHAVING BADLY.

'MORNING, ALL!

HOW ARE . . .

. . . YOU? HOWL!

HEH-HEH!

HUMPH! HOW CHILDISH!

HO-HO!

Later —

OPEN YOUR BOOKS . . .

. . . WAIT!

GROAN! THROWING A TANTRUM AT YOUR AGE, FATTY — HOW CHILDISH!

CHORTLE!

Then —

IIB

OH, NO! WE'LL BE FOR IT NOW!

TEACHER WILL REPORT US TO THE HEAD.

CERTAINLY NOT!

EH? BUT . . . WE'VE BEEN RATHER 'NAUGHTY' ALL DAY!

In the school playground.

AW!

BOOT!

I'LL LOOK FOR IT!

DONK!

LEAP

BASH St. SCHOOL

HO-HO! HE DIDN'T SPOT THAT THE GATES WERE OPEN.

BZZT!
CLICK!
CLICK!
CLICK!

SPIN
SPIN
SPIN

I DON'T THINK THIS IS OUR FOOTBALL!

WHAT IS IT?

SIR! SIR! LOOK AT THIS! A FLOATING FOOTBALL!

WE CAN'T GET IT TO COME DOWN TO THE GROUND FOR OUR GAME!

HUH!

SPIN
SPIN

ONE OF YOUR SILLY TRICKS, EH?

HISTORY

WHAP!

ER . . . WHAT HAVE YOU DONE TO IT?

HISTORY

At school.

GREAT!

WHIRR
ZOOM
SWOOSH

HMM! I WONDER WHO HAS LOST IT?

LOST

IF FOUND RING BEANOTOWN SPACE LAB £1000 REWARD

YES . . . YOUR SATELLITE! ER . . . A REWARD?

ZIP

Very soon.

THANK YOU, SIR!

WHY WAS THE ELEPHANT ARRESTED?

IT WAS TRUNK AND DISORDERLY.

WHY DID THE MANX CAT GO SHOPPING?

IT FANCIED SOME RE-TAIL THERAPY.

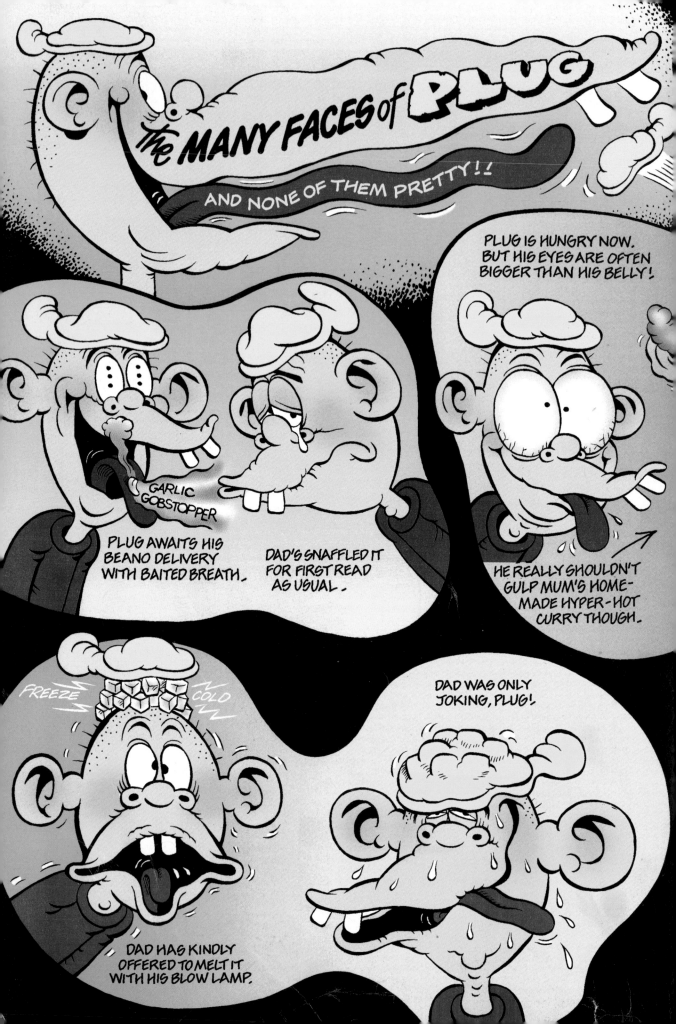

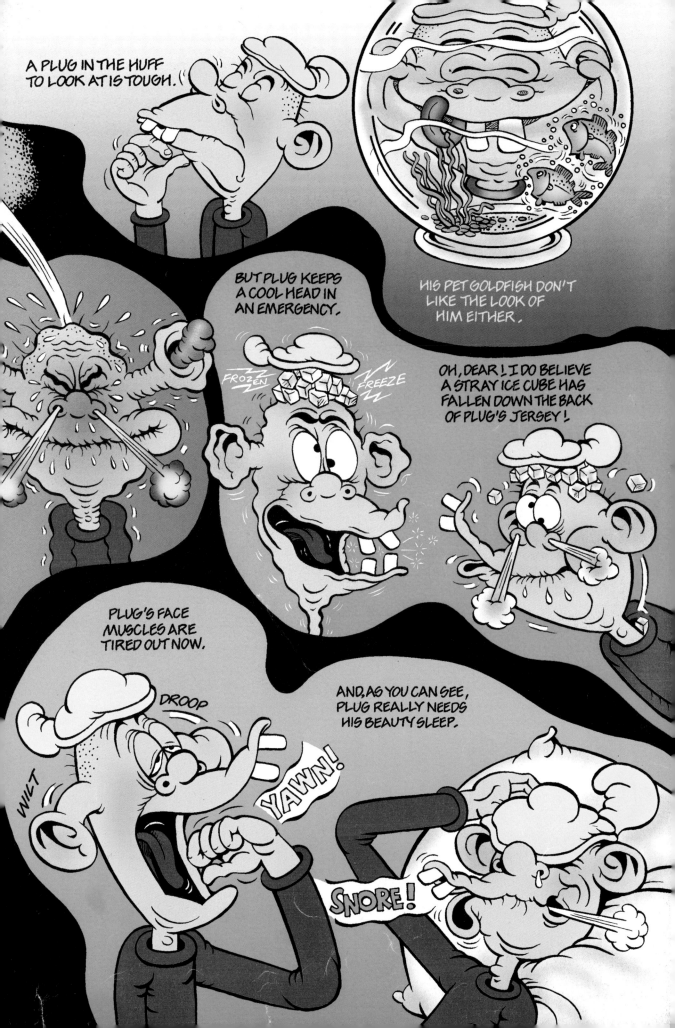

RADIO HA-HA!

COO! RADIO!

COO-EE!

HI, MUM!

SCHOOL

Inside the classroom.

DON'T WORRY — WE'LL CALM HIM DOWN!

BE QUICK!

POLISH

RUB

COMB

SNIP!

STAND ASIDE!

THERE!

CLICK!

TURN

WHERE IS TEACHER?

DON'T KNOW!

TUM... TEE... TUM!

HEADMASTER! WOULD YOU CARE TO STEP IN AT THE LAST MOMENT AND DO THIS LIVE INTERVIEW?

WELL...I... COULDN'T...ER OKAY!

Back in class.

GRR! WHAT A ROTTEN TRICK! LOCKING ME IN THE CUPBOARD! SNARL! YOU'LL PAY FOR THIS!

BUT...BUT IT WASN'T US, SIR! FOR ONCE — WE DIDN'T DO ANYTHING!

DO YOU SING IN THE TOILET?

YES! USUALLY PLOP SONGS!

THEY'RE THE ORCHESTRA PITS

READER'S VOICE— HO-HO! THE HEAD'S NOT PAID THE SCHOOL'S ELECTRICITY BILL AGAIN!

CHEEK! WE'RE AT THE THEATRE! A BIT OF CULTURE FOR THIS LOT! I'VE BROUGHT THEM TO A MOVING PLAY! A WONDERFUL MUSICAL!

WAH!

EEK!

OOH!

WILD THING! YAH! YAH!

THAT'S MUCH BETTER MUSIC!

SO SORRY!

GRR!

Soon—

SAD SONG!

SOB! BLUB! VERY MOVING! SOB!

SAD MUSIC!

SNORE!

BORING!

POP CORN

PHEW! I MUST GET OUT OF HERE TO CONGRATULATE THE CAST! GAG!

... WONDERFUL SHOW ... EXCELLENT ...

THANK YOU!

SSSH!

HEH-HEH!

TIP-TOE

TIP-TOE

WHAT WEARS A WHITE COAT AND HANGS UPSIDE DOWN?

AN UMPIRE BAT!

AHA! THE ORCHESTRA IS ABOUT TO BEGIN. I'D BETTER TAKE A HEAD COUNT. MAKE SURE ALL OF THE KIDS ARE STILL HERE!

PARP! TOOT!

. . . FATTY . . . DANNY . . . TOOTS! WHERE'S TOOTS? NOT IN HER SEAT! EEK!

GASP!

WILD THING! YEAH! TWANG!

AH!

ORCHESTRA PIT

At the interval.

IT'S TIME TO TAKE A BREAK BEFORE THE SECOND PART!

Then —

OOH! AN EVIL PONG! GROO! WHO BROUGHT STINK BOMBS?

HORRIBLE NIFF

NAUSEATING PONG

EH? NO ONE!

OLIVE GAVE US SNACKS FOR THE BREAK!

GAG!

PONG

REVOLTING

GHASTLY

Later.

THINGS WILL BE DIFFERENT IN THE SECOND PART! IT'S CHANGED FROM A 'MOVING PLAY' . . .

. . . TO A 'MOVING TARGET'! HA-HA! FIRE!

SWING

AAAGH! OW!

SPLAT

SPLAT

THROW

WHAT DO YOU CALL A SCOTSMAN IN A COFFIN?

ANOTHER JOCK-IN-THE-BOX!

COME OUT, YOU! YOU'VE CRUSHED MY CAR!

CHORTLE!

I'D LIKE TO HAVE A PLACE IN THIS SCHOOL FOR TEX JR. I'D BE WILLING TO MAKE A SMALL DONATION TO SCHOOL FUNDS!

ER . . . HOW SMALL?

HOW ABOUT THIS FOR STARTERS?

WOW! HE'S IN!

SCHOOL BANK

At the school playing fields.

WHAT'S THAT ROPE AROUND YOUR HAT FOR?

CHOMP!

I USE THIS FOR ROPING ANIMALS!

HA-HA! SORRY! I THOUGHT YOU WERE A FAT PIGGY!

THUD

HUMPH! THAT'S NOT FUNNY! THAT'S OUR PAL!

OO . . . ER!

HE'S NOT THE 'LAUGHING TEXAN' NOW!

WE'RE NOT STAYING HERE!

REVERSE

AT LEAST WE'RE STILL IN FUNDS!

NOT FOR LONG, BUDDIES! 'BYEE!

SUCK

EEK!

SCHOOL BANK

WAH!

CHORTLE! AND TEACHER WILL BE OUT OF OUR WAY FOR A WHILE — REBUILDING HIS CRUSHED CAR!

HO-HO! TOO BAD!

USA

A RIGHT ROYAL RUMPUS

WHERE ARE THE KIDS?

CLASS IIB

HOI! STOP IT!

CRASH

EH?

TO WORK, KIDS! WE MUST CLEAN UP THE SCHOOL!

OKAY! WE'LL HELP!

HOI! WATCH MY UNIFORM!

SWOOSH

SWOOSH

HA-HA!

GROO! ARE YOU DUMPING THIS LOT BEFORE THE ROYAL VISIT?

CHEEK! CERTAINLY NOT!

I'VE LAID ON A STALL! IN CASE ANY OF THE ROYAL PARTY ARE PECKISH!

BY ROYAL APPOINTMENT

WOBBLE

WE'LL SEE!

SLIDE

WHERE'S MY PIZZA?

SNIFF SNIFF

FOUND IT!

CRASH!

ZOOM

LET'S GO — ONE MINUTE LEFT TO THE ROYAL VISIT!

YAHOO!

BASH ST.

BY ROYAL APPOINTMENT

HURRY!

CREAK

YOURS?

OOF!

ER . . . YES! WHAT'S GOING ON?

OH, WE'RE CLEARING ALL RUBBISH FROM THE STREET! THE ROYAL CAR WILL BE PASSING THIS WAY VERY SOON!

ROYAL CAR?

HER?

WE MUST PREPARE BASH STREET SCHOOL FOR THIS PROUD MOMENT! HER ROYAL HIGHNESS MAY STOP LONG ENOUGH TO . . . ER . . . WELL . . .

ARISE, SIR HEAD!

WOW!

PSSST! KEEP THOSE KIDS OUT OF VIEW FOR THE NEXT TEN MINUTES AND THERE'LL BE AN INCREASE OF ONE PENCE A YEAR TO YOUR WAGES!

WOW! YOU'RE ON, YOUR HEADSHIP!

YOU'VE ALL WORKED VERY WELL! TAKE A REST, KIDS!

GOT YOU! STAY IN TILL THE ROYAL CAR'S PASSED!

SIGH! FIVE MINUTE NAP!

In class.

NNNGH! IT'S STUCK! WE'LL MISS THE ROYAL PARTY PASSING!

HMM!

TOPPLE

CRASH!

GET YOUR GRUB HERE MA'AM!

MY NOSH!

BRMM

WHEEE

EH?

SPLUDGE!

SPLAT!

SPLATTER

YOU'VE COST ME A KNIGHTHOOD!

OOYAH! OW!

ONE'S LAUGHING

I ♥ THE BASH STREET KIDS

HE-YAH! HE-YAH!

GREAT VISIT!

WHAT IS THE WORLD'S FASTEST BIRD?

A MISSILE THRUSH.

WHERE DO WOODWORM LAY THEIR EGGS?

IN A NEST OF TABLES.

HEAD LIKES IT HOT

PHEW! IT'S TOO HOT TO GO TO SCHOOL!

LET'S GO INSIDE FOR SOME SHADE!

GASP! IT'S EVEN HOTTER IN HERE!

WHERE'S TEACHER?

PHEW! THIS HEAT'S AWFUL!

OH! I WOULDN'T SAY THAT, TEACHER!

DROOL! IT MEANS I CAN COOK A LITTLE SNACK ON MY DESK LID!

YUM! SMELLS GREAT!

Then.

YUM! CHOMP!

WHEW! IT MUST BE OLIVE COOKING ONE OF HER FAMOUS RED HOT CURRIES AGAIN!

PHEW! LET'S TAKE A LOOK!

AW!

GREEDY PIG!

In the boiler room.

MORE COAL, WINSTON! KEEP IT BURNING!

HAVE YOU GONE MAD, JANITOR? WHY ARE YOU RUNNING THE HEATING SYSTEM SO HIGH?

ER . . . BECAUSE OF THIS NOTE!

PUT ON THE HEATING FULL BLAST AND KEEP IT THERE - OR ELSE FIND ANOTHER JOB.
The Headmaster.

GASP! WHEEZE! TO THE HEAD'S STUDY AND FIND OUT WHY!

WHAT'S GOING ON? WHY IS IT SO HOT IN SCHOOL TODAY?

ER . . . HOT? I HADN'T NOTICED!

GASP! WATER... WATER...

COO! POOR TEACHER! FETCH HIM A DRINK!

GLUG! GLUG!

POUR

HO-HO! YOU MUST HAVE BEEN THIRSTY! WE HAVEN'T CHANGED GOLDIES' WATER THIS YEAR!

EH? YEUCH!

PHOOT!

OW!

SPLASH

NASTY NIFFS!

UNPLEASANT CORDON BLEU PONG!

FOOD SMELL YOU'D RATHER FORGET!

In the kitchen.

NO... NOT ONE OF MY CURRIES! THE FOOD'S DEFROSTING SO FAST...

MELT

FISH

BEANS

FREEZER

MELT

FISH

SAUCES

PRUNE

PONG WHIFF

...IT'LL HAVE TO BE A FISH, SAUSAGE, PRUNE AND BEAN SOUP TODAY! CHORTLE!

HMM! SOUNDS QUITE NICE!

PONG

NIFF

PONG

SAUSAGES

BEANS

FISH

CURRY

PRUNES

BEEF

COD

THE PROBLEM IS THAT THE SCHOOL HEATING'S ON! AT FULL BLAST BY THE FEEL OF IT!

SIZZLE

HEATING? TO THE BOILER ROOM!

AHA! HERE'S THE REASON WHY!

ICE

NO... STAY OUT!

MY... ER... LATEST HOBBY!

SO — THAT'S WHY YOU'VE TURNED THE WHOLE SCHOOL INTO A TROPICAL GREENHOUSE!

CHORTLE!

HA!-HA!

HO-HO!

OUCH! OW! HOWL!

JAB

PRANG

KEEP YOUR COOL, TEACHER! CHORTLE!

WHAT IS THE CLEVEREST FISH IN THE SEA?

THE BRAIN STURGEON.

HARD TO SWALLOW

SIGH! ANOTHER BORING DAY.

LET'S LIVEN IT UP WITH A 'TALL TALE' TELLING COMPETITION.

BAH!

GOOD IDEA!

THIS'LL BE THE PRIZE FOR THE TALLEST TALE TOLD TODAY.

HA-HA! YOU'RE ON!

CHOC BAR

OH . . . SIT DOWN!

HO-HO! NICE ONE, DANNY.

8 6 9 7 5 0

TITTER!

PROD!

HA-HA!

HAND IN YOUR HOMEWORK, TOOTS!

ER . . . A PROBLEM!

TUG

ON MY WAY HERE, A GUST OF WIND BLEW MY JOTTER OUT OF MY HAND . . .

NOT PENCILS, MISS. IT'S FOR MY LUNCHTIME JOB IN BEANOTOWN HOSPITAL.

EEK!

UNZIP

WELL DONE, SMIFFY!

I SAY! VERY ODD!

BAA! BAA!

I DO BRAIN TRANSPLANTS AT LUNCHTIME!

CREAK!

CREAK!

WHAT'S THAT?

WAH! MY SEAT'S BROKEN!

CRASH!

SNAP!

HA-HA!

WHAT DOES A RED SKY AT NIGHT MEAN?

THE SHEPHERD'S COTTAGE IS ON FIRE.

In class —

WHY ARE YOU LATE, YOUNG MAN?

WELL, SIR...

...AN ALIEN SPACECRAFT BEAMED ME UP JUST AT THE CORNER OF ROSE STREET!

AND IT TAKES QUITE A WHILE TO HAVE A TRIP TO MARS AND BACK! AHEM!

WHAT'S THAT, MATE?

...ON TO A PLANE HEADING FOR AUSTRALIA.

I COULD START DIGGING MY WAY DOWN TO OZ AND TRY TO FIND MY JOTTER!

OH, TAKE YOUR SEAT, TOOTS!

CHORTLE!

DO YOU NEED SUCH A BIG PENCIL CASE, SMIFFY?

PENCIL CASE

STRANGE! I ONLY HAD TOAST FOR BREAKFAST.

HO-HO! GOOD TALL TALE, FATTY! ONLY TOAST!

HO-HO!

YOU'VE WON THE TALL TALE CONTEST! HERE'S THE CHOCOLATE!

HA-HA!

BUT...IT'S TRUE... HONEST...

HO-HO! GOOD ONE, FATTY!

CHORTLE! WE COULDN'T TOP THAT ONE, FATTY!

MUNCH! CHOMP! HEH-HEH!

SQUIRT!

MELTED BUTTER

IT'S TRUE, READERS — BUT I DIDN'T SAY JUST HOW MUCH TOAST! CHOMP! HA-HA!

HOW WOULD YOU GET PRIZE DOGS TO FRANCE?

HOVERCRUFTS.

OO... CALM DOWN, CLASS!

I MUST READ THIS! MAYBE SOMETHING IN HERE TO HELP KEEP THEM QUIET!

'WATCHING A TANK OF FISH CAN BE VERY CALMING,' IT SAYS HERE!

CHOMP! CHEW! GNASH!

HA-HA! THAT'S A PIRANHA FISH, FATTY!

WAH!

HO-HO!

SLAP SLAP SLAP

HMM! I WONDER WHY TROPICAL FISH ARE COLOURED THAT WAY? VERY BRIGHT!

WAA!

FLAP-FLAP!

THEY'RE FLYING FISH, SIR!

SPLISH!

COME BACK! BACK INTO THE TANK! COME HERE!

FLAP! FLAP!

Soon —

GASP! WHEEZE! SO, A FISH TANK'S RELAXING, EH? NO CHANCE! WHEW!

WHAT HAS A SCREEN, A KEYBOARD, FOUR PAWS AND A TAIL?

A LAP DOG COMPUTER.

...o, in the afternoon. —

WOW!

I HAD THE PET SHOP SEND A TANK FULL OF FISH AROUND AT LUNCH BREAK!

YUM! I LOVE FISH!

—HALF-EATEN PIE

GLOOP!

SPLASH!

Suddenly —

HOI!

CHOMP!

WHOLLY EATEN PIE

SPLISH!

HA-HA! NOW WE KNOW! SO THEY CAN TELL WHICH TEAM THEY'RE ON!

CHORTLE! BLOWN FOOTBALL!

SHOOT!

PUFF!

Then —

WHAT'S THIS CAGE FOR?

LIFT

Then —

AHA!

SLURP! GLOOP! THE FISH TANK'S A GREAT IDEA . . .

TIP

. . . WITHOUT THE FISH! I GAVE THE FISH BACK TO THE PET SHOP OWNER. IF THE KIDS PLAY UNDERWATER THEY CAN MAKE AS MUCH NOISE AS THEY LIKE! I CAN'T HEAR IT! HAW-HAW-HAW!

GLOOP!

CHOMP!

HMM!

THROW!

WHY DO HILL WALKERS TALK IN THEIR SLEEP?

COS THEY'RE RAMBLERS.

CRICKET BRATS

CRASH

AHA! THOSE BASH STREET KIDS ARE WRECKING THE PLACE AS USUAL!

JUST A MINUTE — WE'RE THOSE BASH STEET KIDS. WHO'S WRECKING THE PLACE THEN?

HA-HA! IT'S TOO EASY FOR YOU LOT TO CHEAT!

WE NEED AN UMPIRE!

SPONGE CAKE BAT

WHO?

AHA! WE HAVE AN UMPIRE!

ON WITH THE MATCH!

OPEN TO BRIBES OF FISH!

I'LL BOWL!

TAP TAP

TUM

HMM! WE'RE BEING MADE TO LOOK FOOLISH!

SWISH

THWACK!

At the teabreak.

WE MAY JUST HAVE A SECRET WEAPON!

SLOO!

EH? YOU WANT ME TO BOWL, DANNY?

YES!

WHAT TYPE OF BALL WILL HE BOWL, HEADMASTER? SPIN? FAST?

ER ... WELL ...

TWIRL!

SPIN!

WHAT HAPPENS IF YOU RUDELY BREAK WIND?

YOU GET A SEVERE GALE WARNING.

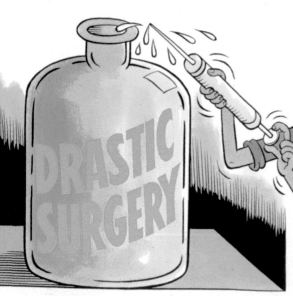

WE'RE NOT GOING TO SCHOOL TODAY! TEACHER WAS RUSHED INTO HOSPITAL LAST NIGHT!

WE'RE GOING THERE TO CHEER HIM UP!

BASH STREET SCHOOL

In hospital.

WHERE ARE YOU, TEACHER?

TEACHER!

COO . . . EE!

NNNGH! IN TO HAVE THIS MORTARBOARD REMOVED?

PULL PUSH

NO . . . I'LL TELL YOU!

KICK!

I WAS HAVING A RELAXING BATH LAST NIGHT AND I . . . ER . . . GOT MY TOE STUCK IN THE TAP!

HO-HO-HO! IS THAT ALL?

WE'LL FIX THAT, SIR!

ZOOM

HOLD IT! WE'LL GIVE IT ONE MORE TRY WITH THIS GREASE GUN!

MORE GREASE ON IT, DANNY!

SQUIRT

SPLAT

SPLOT

One tug later.

YAHOO! DONE IT!

WHEE

Later.

DOH! WHAT HAPPENED?

WE HAVE GOOD NEWS AND BAD NEWS, SIR!

WHAT DO YOU CALL AN EXTINCT FOOTBALLER?

RONALDODO!

TRYING TO HIDE, EH?

HO-HO!

HUMPH! WHAT DO YOU LOT WANT?

SHAKING WITH FEAR

WHAT A CHEEK! WE'VE BROUGHT YOU PRESENTS!

HUH! I SUPPOSE IT WAS KIND OF YOU TO COME!

← LOLLY STICKS

STING!

LAXATIVES

FRUIT BASKET

WHAT ARE YOU IN FOR, SIR?

PLASTIC SURGERY?

OO . . . YES! YOU COULD DO WITH SEVERAL INCHES CHOPPED OFF THIS! HA-HA-HA!

TUG

NO . . . STOP!

RUMBLE

PREPARE GOWNS, INSTRUMENTS, PATIENT . . . LIGHTS . . . CURTAIN UP — WE'RE ON, KIDS! HEH!

NO . . . !

THEATRE 13

CRASH!

THUD!

ZOOM

RUMBLE

HEH-HEH! STOP! HO-HO!

HMM! IT'S STUCK FAST! ONLY ONE THING FOR IT . . .

GIGGLE GAS

. . . CUT OFF THE TOE!

HA-HA-HA! GIGGLE! STOP!

THE GOOD NEWS IS — THE TAP'S OFF YOUR TOE . . .

. . . THE BAD NEWS IS — YOU'VE GOT AN EMPTY GREASE GUN STUCK ON YOUR TOE!

THE TAP'S NOW ON YOUR NOSE! THAT'S WHERE IT LANDED WHEN IT SLIPPED OFF YOUR TOE!

GRRRR!

GRRR! WAIT TILL I CATCH YOU!

HEH-HEH! IN OUR OPINION — YOU SHOULDN'T BE UP ON YOUR FEET SO SOON AFTER A MAJOR OPERATION!

WARDS 22-46 →

CLUNK! CLUNK!

WHAT DO ITALIANS PUT ON THEIR TOAST?

NAPLES SYRUP!

TIME FOR A LAUGH

9.30 a.m.

GRRR! WHAT TIME DO YOU CALL THIS?

ER... BIG HAND PAST THE OTHER ONE!

TWO BANANAS PAST A PLUM 'IN MY PLAYTIME SNACK!

AN ALARM CLOCK — AND IT'S VERY ALARMED BY THE SIGHT OF YOU!

TRING!! TRING!

TAKE OFF YOUR SHOES AND WE'LL VISIT THE VERY ACCURATE TIMEPIECE WHICH THE WORLD SETS THEIR CLOCKS BY!

TUG
TUG
TUG
PONK

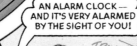

WHAT TYPE OF CLOCK IS THIS?

YIKES!

SPLURT!

BITE

HO!! I LOST SOME JAM THERE! CAN YOU SCRAPE IT OFF, MISTER?

SNARL!

STUCK

WHIRRR

SPIN

So, in China.

BONE CHINA RADIO
BONG BONG

WOK

In U.S.A.

HAMBURGER RADIO
BONG BONG

OIL

In Australia.

BOOMERANG RADIO
BONG BONG

At the North Pole.

ICE-BLOCK RADIO
BONG BONG

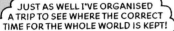

JUST AS WELL I'VE ORGANISED A TRIP TO SEE WHERE THE CORRECT TIME FOR THE WHOLE WORLD IS KEPT!

HUH! I WISH THE HEAD WOULD BOOK A BUS RATHER THAN ME USING MY CAR!

OLD SKINFLINT!

COO! A DAY OUT!

SUPER!

CHUG!

PHUT!

CHUG!

TISK! YOU'RE ONE AND A HALF SECONDS LATE, TEACHER!

AHEM, SORRY!

CLOCK SPRING TROUSERS

HO-HO! TISK! TISK! LATE, SIR?

YES! ALL TYPES OF CLOCKS HERE!

GRANDPA AND GRANNY CLOCK

CUKOO!

SEAGULL CLOCK

OSTRICH CLOCK

YOU DIDN'T HAVE TO TAKE YOUR SOCKS OFF, SMIFFY!

I DIDN'T — THEY FELL APART!

PONG HUM

WHIFF

GASH!

THIS IS THE WORLD TIMEPIECE! SSSH! NOTHING MUST UPSET THE FINE BALANCE OF THIS CLOCK!

TICK

TOCK

TICK

TICK

TOCK

RUMBLE

SLURP! I'M PECKISH!

JAM DOUGH-NUTS

Then —

EH? TWENTY SEVEN O'CLOCK?

BONG BONG BONG BONG BONG BONG

TWENTY EIGHT O'CLOCK?

BONG BONG BONG BONG BONG BONG BONG

TWENTY NINE?

BONG BONG BONG BONG

WHAT'S HAPPENING?

BONG BONG BONG BONG BONG BONG BONG

MELT

Back at the clock works.

GRRR! YOU'VE RUINED MY PRICELESS CLOCK! SNARL!

BOINNG BOINNG BOINNG

OOOYAH!

EEK!

WAH!

HA-HA!

OOYAH!

RADIO MIKE

CLAP

PHOTO SHOCK

SIGH! WHAT CAN HAPPEN TODAY?

IIB

Suddenly —

WOW!

FLASH!

CAN'T SEE!

MY EYES!

... IN MY TEACUP?

HA-HA!

SHAMPOO

MUNCH! CHOMP! MY JACKET DIDN'T LOOK AS IF IT WAS FITTING PROPERLY! I'LL HAVE TO FILL IT OUT A BIT! GOBBLE!

FLASH

BURP! OOPS!

RIP

HA-HA!

HOLD IT!

A few seconds later.

HOI! YOU LOT — STAND STILL!

MOVE OVER!

STOP PUSHING!

STAY AWAY!

I'LL GET YOU!

FLASH

Later.

I SUPPOSE IT'S A GOOD LIKENESS!

WOULD YOU LIKE A COPY, READERS?

DOH!

CUT ROUND THE DOTTED LINES AND STICK IT ON A PIECE OF CARD!

HMM! YES — A GOOD LIKENESS!

SCRAPE

WHO INVENTED SMELLY CHEESE?

GORDON ZOLA!

THE BASH STREET KIDS AND TEACHER

WHY DID SMIFFY SLEEP UNDER THE BED?

COS HE'S A LITTLE POTTY!

WE'RE HOLDING A 'STARS IN DISGUISE' CONTEST!

BUT ANYONE WHO'S NOT VERY GOOD GETS GONGED OFF THE STAGE!

BOING!

TO BEGIN THE CONTEST, FATTY IS . . . KING HENRY THE EIGHTH!

STAGE

NOW, STOP ME IF YOU'VE HEARD THIS ONE BEFORE, BUT THERE WERE THESE . . .

CAREFUL, HERBERT

YIKES!

WHAT'S A YIKE?

NOW DANNY IS — PAUL DANIELS!

YOU'RE GOING TO LIKE THIS TRICK. NOT A LOT, BUT YOU'LL LIKE IT!

I'M GOING TO MAKE FATTY VANISH!

BRING ME BACK IN TIME FOR TEA, DANNY!

CLOSE

TAP TAP

One second later

HEY — PRESTO! FATTY'S GONE!

GOSH! HOW DID HE DO THAT?

REGRETS, I'VE HAD A LOT, SINCE JOINING BASH STREET, TOO MANY TO MENTION. BUT THEN AGAIN, I'VE HAD MY HIGHS, EXAMINATIONS AND DETENTIONS . . .

GET OFF!

BADOING!

AND FINALLY — TOOTS AS MADONNA!

LEAP

STAGE

TEACHER DON'T PREACH, 'COS I'M ALWAYS IN TROUBLE YOU OFTEN COME IN LATE, WITH A FACE FULL OF STUBBLE!

WHEEEE!

RUBBISH!

MEOW!

STAGE

DROP

HUH! THE CONTESTANTS WERE SO POOR, I DON'T KNOW WHO TO GIVE THIS TROPHY TO!